Poems for My Mom

by

Amy H. Reynolds

Dorrance Publishing Co
585 Alpha Drive
Pittsburgh, PA 15238
Visit our website at www.dorrancebookstore.com

ISBN: 979-8-89027-369-7
eISBN: 979-8-89027-867-8

Endora

Fur of gray,

Eyes so green,

Face so gentle with

Your paws of white.

You look at me

As if to say,

I love you

Now let's go play.

We play with almost anything,

Because all you want,

Are a few moments of my time?

Endora, my dear cat.

Samantha

Your beginnings were rocky

But your life now is so sweet

You can brighten our day

With just a glance

Your face is so revealing

Of all that you conceal

You can't imagine

Just how much you brighten our day

Much more living

Much more warm

Our lives will never be the same

Because you are part of us

Rain

Rain falls gently

From the sky

Glistening as it

Hits the ground

Some may dread you,

Some may complain,

Others may look forward

to your approach.

While others may be amazed

At how you fall from the sky

But to me your presence makes

his presence clearer.

Sunshine

Your presence is felt

by all around.

By the warmth and power

that you abound.

Your presence gives life

to all the living.

How wise, wonderful, and giving.

The flowers, the trees

The animals and beasts

All owe you their life

Yet some fail to see

How amazing your

power and grace.

Sleep

You come at night

Silent and still

Sometimes we greet

You with anticipation

But sometimes with fear and anxiety

You know this and

Still you wait

Until we relax

And greet you

with ease and grace.

Peace

Always sought

Never truly attained

All mankind would love to know

How to keep you for their own

You come to us

When we need you the most

Yet someone always

Seeks to turn you away

As if to say,

"You are

Not needed today."

How can we keep you

around when all else fails?

Maybe we are not truly

ready for your presence.

Love

You fill my heart

With joy

Yet my heart cries

out for more.

Am I greedy

or merely human?

Some seek you

Always but never catch you.

Some catch you yet then

Turn you away.

I truly enjoy having

You in my heart

But hope I never

Run out of room for more.

Voices

Many voices sing

Many voices scream.

All who speak have the right

To use their voice

Yet some don't know

when to stop.

"We have the right," they say.

"This is true," we reply.

"But we also have rights."

Perhaps the rights of all

Should be known

To those who seek to know.

I have a voice too

But choose to share mine

With those that seek to listen.

Perhaps you should too.

Silence

Silence falls across the town.

How still, how peaceful, how serene.

You seem to be lost in our lives.

Yet all who live

would love to see you.

If not forever

But just for awhile.

Just to have a moment to think.

Just to have some time

To reflect on how precious

Silence truly is.

Dream world

How sweet you look

cuddled up in a ball.

You seem so happy

lost in another world.

Your dreams take over

Your body is still.

Your eyes are shut.

Your hands are limp.

I hasten to wake you

But it is time to go.

You now are rested

And ready to play.

Music

Some prefer opera

Some prefer jazz.

I prefer this and that

You like them all too.

Our tastes are alike

Our views are too.

Yet sometimes I wonder

just what to make of you.

You like the rain but

I like the thunder.

Will we ever agree?

Over time we will see.

Faith

I believed in you once.

But in the blink of an eye, you

seemed to disappear.

In one day, I began

To question how one so

Wonderful could cause such pain.

My heart was broken

His heart was too.

But together we shall

Find our way back to you.

Exodus

Our people were oppressed

and worked so very hard.

Their leader was a simple man

Yet you choose him to lead them

to a land of milk and honey.

You told him to take them

To the Promised Land

For this was their destiny.

Our people today are still

Searching for a land

where their views are accepted.

Where are their dreams to be realized?

Is this too much to ask?

ILEAN RENE SLACTER
יטא רייוועל
JUN. 18, 1936
NOV. 16, 2022
BELOVED MOTHER AND GRANDMOTHER

My cats

Ferocious little lions

Of this I have four

You stand so bravely

Yet you are so kind.

You always know just what to do

When I am so sad and blue

You rub your face

Across my hand

And softly say

"I don't care what you do."

"I will always love you."

Why I love you

As I sit and wonder

Why things happen

I am reminded

Why I love you.

I love you for your eyes

I love you for your face.

I love you for your hands

I love you for your smile.

But most of all

I love you for your patience

I love you for your grace

I love you for your wit

And I love you for your charm.

David, my dear

You are so patient,

David, my dear.

Of this I truly feel.

Your kindness I never doubt

Of this I must confess.

Your heart is so big

for me and ours.

This does always amaze me.

How someone so selfless

Did come my way

that wonderful day in May.

I am truly blessed.

Cats

You seem so aloof

Yet we know better.

You're so very sweet

and so very funny.

Others don't get it that

We love you so.

Cats aren't pets.

They are hardly worth it.

We know so much better.

You've added so much to our lives.

We can't imagine our lives

without you.

And yet it may be true.

We don't "own" you,

You own us.

This we know is true.

A Hero

A hero is one that truly knows

how to inspire us as we grow.

He was a hero

Because he lived in a time

of war and peace.

His life ended much too soon.

Who knows what our lives

Would be if only he had chosen

to see and not to act.

What lessons to learn?

What acts to imitate?

We should not at all

Instead, we should follow

Our own hearts and be a hero

to someone else—ourselves.

Hope

I still believe that I can do it

though some may doubt me.

I just have to prove it.

My heart has been broken.

My will has been shot.

I have your love as a token.

My eyes are still red.

My heart still hurts.

I have to fight to get out of bed.

But with your love

And with your support

And help from above.

I can get through this

I know I can.

I just need a kiss.

My love

You were my first love.

I cared for you so much.

You were not real

I loved to see your smile.

Your eyes were big and black.

Your eyes were round and plastic.

I carried you everywhere.

Just hearing your voice

made me go crazy.

Now I am grown.

I have a new love.

You're still very special—a

friend from Disney.

A dream

I had a dream last night

That you were not gone

You had not taken flight

We were with you and not alone.

At last, sadly I awoke

You had left us.

It was not a joke.

This time we did not fuss.

We said goodbye.

We shed a tear.

We waved goodbye.

No cries did we hear.

Our hearts are heavy.

But this time we know.

Our tears are many.

It is indeed time for you to go.

Life

Life is full of valleys.

Sometimes it seems so hard.

Yet we always try

to move on in our lives.

Life is like a ball game.

Some hits and some misses.

We must always still try

To do our best at all times

even though it is tough.

It really is worth it.

The thrill is hard to beat.

Until you find it, you

never really compete.

Today 1

Today I may cry

This too will pass

As time goes by

My heart feels like it is made of glass

Tomorrow will bring healing

It just takes time.

I can't fight the feeling

So I write this for me.

With every passing day,

With every passing month

Your memory will not go away

On this I can count on.

Today 2

Time goes by ever so slowly

I try not to cry.

With each passing day,

People ask how I'm doing.

Sometimes I don't know what to say.

I think of you often and

Sometimes I wonder.

My heart skips a little

As I hear thunder.

The days get shorter

The nights are long

Sometimes I wonder

As I hear a song I wonder

Where you are.

Are you really gone?

My mind plays a game

This isn't real

I hear your name

Come from my lips

But no one answers.

My spirit takes a dip.

Voices

Many voices sing

Many voices scream.

All who speak have the right

To use their voice

Yet some don't know

when to stop.

"We have the right," they say.

"This is true," we reply.

"But we also have rights."

Perhaps the rights of all

Should be known

To those who seek to know.

I have a voice too

But choose to share mine

With those that seek to listen.

Perhaps you should too.

9 7 9 8 8 9 0 2 7 3 6 9 7